1-08

AROUND THE WORLD WITH MONEY

MONEY POWER

Jason Cooper

Rourke
Publishing LLC
Vero Beach, Florida 32964

www.rourkepublishing.com

PHOTO CREDITS: © Corel Corporation; © East Coast Studios; © James P. Rowan; © Lynn M. Stone; © Elwin Trump; © Oscar C. Williams; © The Smithsonian Institution National Numismatic Collection

Cover Photo: *Much of the world's currency is printed in bright colors.*

Editor: Frank Sloan

Cover design by Nicola Stratford

Library of Congress Cataloging-in-Publication Data

Cooper, Jason
    Around the world with money / Jason Cooper
       p. cm. — (Money power)
    Includes bibliographical references and index.
    Summary: Discusses currency used around the world, featuring the money of the United States, Canada, Europe, Japan, and China.
    ISBN 1-58952-212-5
    1. Money—Juvenile literature. [1. Money.] I. Title.

HG221.5 .C665 2002
332.4—dc21
                                      2001048912

Printed in the USA

CG/CG

TABLE OF CONTENTS

MONEY IN DIFFERENT PLACES

Most countries make their own money, or **currency**. They use their own written language, pictures, and **symbols** on their currency.

Each country decides its own basic unit of money, too. In the United States, the U.S. dollar is the basic currency. In Canada, it is the Canadian dollar. In Mexico the peso is the basic money unit.

Many kinds of money are used in different parts of the world.

MONEY IN EUROPE

In Europe, the situation is different. European countries tend to be smaller than many American states. Europeans easily travel between one European country and another. But each country has always had its own currency. An Italian traveling in Germany would have to exchange lire for German deutsche marks. And before the day's end, that person might have to make exchanges in other countries!

Many banks display the exchange rates of money from other countries.

FOREIGN CURRENCY EXCHANGE

	Country	Rate
	AUSTRALIA	·7041
	CANADA	·6938
	DENMARK	·1636
	FINLAND	·2046
	FRANCE	·1844
	GERMANY	·6401
	ITALY	·00059
	JAPAN	·00887
	MEXICO	·1213
	SPAIN	·00748
	SWEDEN	·1327
	UNITED KINGDOM	1·4558

THE EURO

In 2002 much European money changed. Twelve European countries agreed to share one currency, called the **euro**. Now a traveler in those 12 European countries needs just one currency instead of 12.

The 12 countries using euros are Austria, Belgium, Finland, France, Germany, Greece, Ireland, Italy, Luxembourg, the Netherlands, Portugal, and Spain. Several other European countries, including Great Britain, decided to keep their own currencies.

The euro became the currency in 12 European countries in 2002.

TRADE BETWEEN COUNTRIES

Businesses in one country often buy and sell goods from another country. This kind of **commerce**, or business, between countries is called foreign trade. The United States, for example, sells great amounts of wheat to other countries.

Goods traded between countries can be paid for with money or other goods. The trading of goods for goods, instead of money, began hundreds of years ago. In foreign trade, it is still a way to do business.

Ships with products from all over the world are unloaded at this busy seaport.

People can buy handmade goods at street markets in many countries.

Many Mexican vendors will accept U.S. and local currency for their goods.

MONEY IN THE UNITED STATES

The value of money in America and elsewhere is set by governments, not by the size of the bill. All U.S. paper money, or bank notes, is the same size. They are printed in amounts of 1, 2, 5, 10, 20, 50, and 100 dollars. A $1 bill is the same size as a $100 bill.

The dollar equals 100 cents. Each cent is called a penny. A nickel is worth 5 cents. A dime is worth 10 cents, and a quarter is worth 25 cents.

The U.S. $1 bill has the same value as 100 pennies.

MONEY IN CANADA

Canadian bills are printed in amounts of 1, 2, 5, 10, 20, 50, 500, and 1,000 dollars.

Like the U.S., Canada makes several different coins. One of the most commonly used is the "looney," a $1 coin that has the picture of a **loon** on it.

Canadian coins are officially 1-, 5-, 10-, 25-, and 50-cent pieces. But Canadians usually call them pennies, nickels, dimes, quarters, and half dollars.

The Canadian "looney" coin, which shows a loon on its face

Fort Resolution
Eskimo Point
Fort Smith
Fitzgerald
Fort Chipewyan
Fond du Lac
Uranium City
Ft. Vermilion
Athabasca
Wollaston L.
Churchill
Brochet
Cree L.
Reindeer Lake
Peace River
Fort McMurray
Bird
York Factory
Lynn Lake
Gillam
Churchill
Nelson
Flin Flon
La Ronge
Athabasca
SASKATCHEWAN
Lloydminster
N. Battlef
CANADA
DIX
TEN
CANADA
LA BIBLIOTHÈQUE DU
THE LIBRARY OF PARLIAMENT

MONEY IN MEXICO

Mexico's currency is based on the peso. The peso is familiar to many Americans who spend time in Mexico.

The peso takes its name from the old Spanish dollars. When Spain conquered Mexico and much of Central and South America, it introduced the peso.

The value of the peso against the American or Canadian dollar changes every day. In late 2001 one peso was worth about one American dime.

This Mexican bill is worth 2000 pesos.

MONEY IN OTHER PLACES

Scandinavia is a region of several countries in northern Europe. Currency names in some of the countries there have different spellings, but the words mean the same. For instance, money from Denmark and Norway is krone. Money in Sweden is krona. The words mean "crown."

China's basic money unit is the yuan. Japan's is the yen. Both currencies are becoming more and more familiar to Americans. China and Japan are among America's largest trading partners.

Sweden was the first European country to make paper money.

SVERIGES
RIKSBANK

50

FEMTIO KRONOR

1965 F
B 699803

GUSTAV III 1771–1792

EXCHANGING MONEY

Each nation's basic unit of money has a different **value**. One British pound, for example, is worth more than one American dollar. One American dollar is worth more than one Canadian dollar. But values of currencies change, at least slightly, each day.

Most businesses in the United States and elsewhere do not accept **foreign** currency. People who travel to other countries need to exchange money. An American traveling to Great Britain would trade American dollars for British pounds at a British bank or at a **currency exchange**.

GLOSSARY

commerce (KOHM URSE) — business

currency (KER en see) — money, especially paper money

currency exchange (KER en see IKS chaynj) — place of business that can change one nation's money into another's

euro (YUR oh) — new money being used in 12 European countries

foreign (FOHR en) — from another country

loon (LOON) — a large diving bird that nests in Canada and the northern United States

symbols (SIM buhlz) — those objects, such as a flag, that stand for something more than the objects themselves

value (VAL yoo) — the amount of money something is worth or that people will pay for it

INDEX

Further Reading

Lewis, Brenda R. *Focus on Coins and Currency*. DIANE Publishing, 1999

Websites To Visit

http://www.xe.net/ucc
http://www.moneyfactory.com

About The Author

Jason Cooper has written several children's books about a variety of topics for Rourke Publishing, including recent series *China Discovery* and *American Landmarks*. Cooper travels widely to gather information for his books. Two of his favorite travel destinations are Alaska and the Far East.